NEADS (National Education for Assistance Dog Services, also known as Dogs for Deaf and Disabled Americans) of Princeton, Massachusetts, a non-profit organization established in 1976, places specially trained service dogs to provide freedom, physical autonomy, and relief from social isolation to their human partners. In 2006, NEADS pioneered a program, Canines for Combat Veterans, geared to place dogs with veterans of the Iraq and Afghanistan wars. In 2009, the Trauma Assistance Dog (TAD) Program developed as part of Canines for Combat Veterans to place trained service dogs with veterans suffering from combat-related post-traumatic stress (PTSD). Encouraging results show that dogs help veterans with PTSD to cope with their symptoms.

A portion of proceeds from sales of this book will be donated to Canines for Combats Veterans. To learn more about NEADS, please visit www.neads.org.

Only Daddy's Dog

written by Cynthia Crosson

illustrated by Carole Williams

Haley's • Athol, MA

Haley's
488 South Main Street
Athol, MA 01331
haley.antique@verizon.net
800.215.8805

International Standard Book Number 978-0-9897667-2-2
    trade paperback
International Standard Book Number 978-0-9897667-3-9
    hardcover
International Standard Book Number 978-1-884540-95-0
    eBook

Copy edited by Helen Hills.

Only Daddy's Dog was written for the
Trauma Assistance Dog Program • Canines for Combat Veterans
NEADS (National Education for Assistance Dog Services, also known as
Dogs for Deaf and Disabled Americans)

for our veterans and their families
who have given so much

I like to look at pictures of Daddy and me. When I was a baby, Daddy held me in his strong arms. When I learned to walk, Daddy held my hand. We played ball together, and he read me stories.

At the playground, Daddy pushed me on the swings.

Before Daddy went to war, he was my best friend.

One day Mommy and Daddy told me that Daddy was going away for a while. He was going to a place called Iraq where people were fighting a war. Daddy said that the president of the United States told him he had to go and that it was a very important job. They needed his help. Mommy explained that other daddies and even mommies would also be going to war, too.

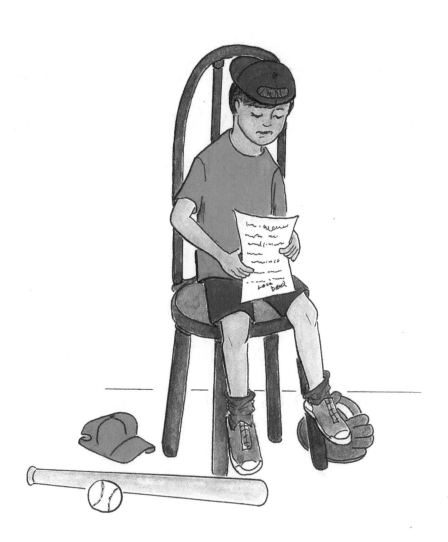

After Daddy went away, we got letters from him and sometimes e-mails. But I missed my Daddy. Playing ball wasn't much fun, and I missed Daddy telling me stories.

Then one day Mommy took me on her lap, and I could see the tears run down her cheeks. She told me that Daddy had been hurt and he was in the hospital in another state. Mommy needed to go to see him. I wanted to go, too, but Mommy told me that I couldn't yet. But Grandma would stay with me until they could come home. I liked being with Grandma, but I missed my Mommy and my Daddy.

But when Mommy came home, Daddy wasn't with her. She told me that he would be home in two months. I was so excited, and I counted off the days on the calendar. And then the day came when Mommy went to pick up Daddy and bring him home. She said that they would get home late and I needed to go to bed, but in the morning Daddy would be here.

I didn't think I would sleep, but I must have because I woke up to a beautiful sunny morning. I jumped out of bed and ran to Mommy and Daddy's bedroom. There was only one person in the bed, and I thought "He didn't come!" But then I saw Mommy tiptoe in. She was already up. Sure enough, Daddy was there in bed. I was so excited that I was going to jump on him like I used to do. But Mommy told me that I had to be quiet and let Daddy sleep.

"I'll go make breakfast while Daddy sleeps," Mommy said. "Why don't you play until it's ready." Mommy also explained that we had to be very quiet.

As she made breakfast, I thought about what she had said. And I built a big tower thinking about all the things I would tell Daddy when he woke up.

I was so busy that I didn't even hear Daddy when he got up until he came up behind me and said "Hello, Son. What are you building there?"

I was so excited that I rushed to hug him, knocking over my tower with a huge crash!

Daddy screamed and put his hands over his ears. Then he pushed me away and went back into the bedroom and slammed the door.

"What did I do?" I cried.

"It's okay," Mommy told me. She told me that Daddy was still healing and we had to be patient. She explained that Daddy might seem different to me.

From then on, Daddy yelled at Mommy a lot and made her cry. It made me cry, too. And when he wasn't yelling, Daddy sat in his room. He didn't want to go out or play with me. He didn't want to read me stories. I wondered where my *real* Daddy had gone.

One day, Mommy took Daddy and me to a lady, Dr. Cope, who said that she was a counselor who helped families like ours. Daddy had his own counselor, too, but this lady wanted to see all of us together. Dr. Cope told me that she thought that Daddy should apply for a special dog that would help him feel better. A dog! I was so happy.

"But it won't be a family dog," she explained. "It will be a dog to help Daddy to get well. It would not be my dog or Mommy's dog. It would be only Daddy's dog. I wasn't sure how I felt about that!

Mommy drove Daddy to a place called NEADS to talk with the people there about the dog. I thought they would come home with the dog, but they didn't. Mommy told me that Daddy would go to NEADS for two weeks of training with his dog, but he would bring the dog home to meet all of us on the weekend in between. When training was finished then the dog would come home for good with Daddy. I asked if I could go to help Daddy with his dog too, but Mommy said that it was only for Daddy and his dog to learn and get used to working together.

On the day that Daddy came home, I waited by the window. And I saw them come up the walk. It was a big black dog with floppy ears and a wagging tail.

"His name is Hero," Mommy told me. I wanted to run up and hug Hero.

A dog!! I had always wanted a dog. But then I remembered what Mommy had said. This was only Daddy's dog.

The next morning, Daddy got up early instead of sleeping late as he had been doing. "I have to take Hero out for a walk," he told me. I think he sounded happier.

"Can I go?" I asked.

"Sure," said Daddy. And Hero and Daddy and I walked around the neighborhood. It was the first time that I had been out with my Daddy in a long, long time.

That afternoon, I watched Daddy throw the ball for Hero in the back yard.

"Can I go out and throw the ball too?" I asked Mommy.

"Maybe sometime Daddy will let you. But let Daddy and Hero get used to each other now."

But it was fun to watch my Daddy and his dog. He laughed, and I could see the Daddy that I used to have.

A few days later, I was trying to read a book, but it had some really big words in it. I sat on the floor right near Hero pretending to read the book to him. When I stumbled over some of the words, Hero just looked up at me like he wanted to help. And then Daddy smiled at us and said "Here, let me read it to both of you."

So I put my arm around Hero, and we listened to Daddy read the book to us.

Hero was always with Daddy. He went to the store with us. He went for walks with us. He slept by Daddy's bed, and he sat by Daddy's chair. Daddy was different with Hero around. He got up early, and he stayed up all day. He went out more and seemed more cheerful. He didn't seem to need Mommy to do everything for him. And he didn't spend time just staying in his room and not talking to anyone. I really liked having Hero around. Even if he was only Daddy's dog.

I told everyone at school all about Hero, and my teacher said that I should do a report about Daddy's dog. She thought maybe Daddy could bring him in and show the class. I said I'd do the report. It would be fun, but I told her that I didn't think Daddy could come in. He was just too busy, I said. I didn't tell them that Daddy was afraid to go into crowds, and he'd never come.

Mommy and I took some pictures of Hero, and I made a scrapbook about how Daddy got him from NEADS. Mommy said that it looked so good that she bet that I would get an A. The next day, when it was time for me to give my report, I was really nervous. But when I started showing the pictures, there were lots of questions.

"What's it like to have an assistance dog?" someone asked. "Does he look like just any dog?"

"Well," I began. "Hero looks like any dog, but he's special." I didn't know what else to say.

And suddenly the door opened and a black head peered in. And then Daddy was there with Hero.

"This is my Dad!" I cried and ran to hug him. And everyone clapped, and Daddy didn't even seem upset at all the noise that would have frightened him before he got Hero.

"You worked so hard on your scrapbook," he said. "But I thought that everyone would like to meet Hero and see what he can do."

And he showed them how Hero could open doors and turn lights on and off and bring Daddy things that he dropped. And Daddy had Hero say hello to everyone. I knew everyone would be talking about my report for a long time.

And when he had greeted all the other kids, Hero came over and licked my face.

"You know, " I told him. "You may be only Daddy's dog, but you're special to me too . . . Because of you, I have my Daddy back again."

And Hero wagged his tail, as if he understood.

Cynthia Crosson

About the Author

Cynthia Crosson, Ed.D, is the psychiatric consultant for the Trauma Assistance Dog Program (TAD) that trains service dogs for veterans with post-traumatic stress (PTSD) and traumatic brain injury. TAD is one of the offerings of NEADS (National Education for Assistance Dog Services, also known as Dogs for Deaf and Disabled Americans)/Canines for Combat Veterans. Dr. Crosson was the co-developer of the TAD program and is on the board of directors of NEADS. In addition, she is involved in organizations that help returning veterans and their families.

Dr. Crosson is a nationally known writer in the field of child abuse, child welfare, and PTSD. She is pastor of the First Congregational Church, UCC of Whately, Massachusetts. She is also a retired college professor. She resides with her family in central Massachusetts.

Carole Williams

About the Illustrator

Drawing and painting have been lifelong hobbies for Carole, who says she can spend hours doing a dog portrait, creating a painting from a photo she has taken somewhere, or illustrating just something that comes to mind.

Not having any formal art training, she says she has been blessed over the years to be working in some area of art. Her first job was as a plate artist for the Norcross greeting card company in New York City. Later she became a technical illustrator for Airborne Instruments on Long Island. She also worked for and retired from IBM as an illustrator/designer.

After retirement Carole painted wall murals for clients. She also enjoyed doing decorative painting on furniture. Now living in the Adirondack Mountains of New York, she has added gourd projects, cane making, and wood burning to her artistic repertoire.

Author's Acknowledgments

There are many whose efforts and support go into the writing of any book. I would like to thank my "trauma assistance-dog team," Kathy Foreman and trainers Brian Jennings and Erin Wylie, who not only birthed the program with me but continue to work diligently to meet the needs of veterans and their families. Our wonderful working relationship has brought us through many challenges. My thanks to Christy Bassett who also trained, to Sue Berry for her wonderful administrative assistance, and to the NEADS staff who have helped in many ways. I appreciate the support of fellow members of the board of directors and especially Anita Migday, who found such a great illustrator. Thanks to my granddaughter Ruby who "proofed" the book with discerning six-year-old eyes. And especially to all the veterans and their families who have taught us so much.

Illustrator's Acknowledgments

Thanks to my husband Robert for his ever present patience and encouragement for all my art endeavors. Also I wish to thank Anita Migday, who is on the board of NEADS, for putting me in touch with Cynthia Crosson who graciously gave me the privilege of creating the illustrations for her book.

Colophon

Text and titles for *Only Daddy's Dog* are set in ITC Stone Sans.

In 1987, Sumner Stone completed his designs for the Stone type family. ITC Stone solves the problem of mixing different styles of type on the same page. Most combined type styles, because they aren't designed to work together, often have radically different characteristics such as cap heights, stem weights, and proportions. The ITC Stone family consists of three subfamilies, Serif, Sans, and Informal, each consisting of three weights plus matching italics. As a large integrated family, the Stone types can be mixed successfully with each other in newsletters, business correspondence, books, and packaging. ITC Stone Sans is a modern version of the "humanistic" sans-serif subcategory.

In 1992, John Renner finished designing phonetic companion faces for ITC Stone Sans and ITC Stone Serif. They contain the linguistic symbols used by the International Phonetic Association, comprising more than 300 letters and diacritical marks, both historical and official. These typefaces are appropriate for dictionaries, language guides, linguistic texts, or wherever else spoken sounds need to be typographically represented.

The font for the cover title is Hobo Standard. Hobo is a sans serif typeface. It is unique in having virtually no straight lines and no descenders. It was created by Morris Fuller Benton and issued by American Type Founders in 1910. Digital versions of this face are often found in Mac OS and Microsoft Windows systems.

CPSIA information can be obtained at www.ICGtesting.com
Printed in the USA
BVOW11s2059151014

371022BV00003B/4/P